CAF HOW TO APPLY TO A GRANT MAKING TRUST

A guide for fundraisers

ANNE VILLEMUR

©1996 Anne Villemur

Published by Charities Aid Foundation
Kings Hill
West Malling
Kent ME19 4TA

Editor   Caroline Hartnell

Design and production   Eugenie Dodd Typographics

Printed and bound in Great Britain by Bell & Bain Limited, Glasgow

A catalogue record for this book is available from the British Library.

ISBN 1-85934-033-4

All rights reserved: no part of this work may be reproduced in any form, by mimeograph or any other means, without permission in writing from the publisher.

Telephone   +44 (0) 1732 520000
Fax   +44 (0) 1732 520001
E-mail   Cafpubs@CAF.charitynet.org

CAF's web page:
http://www.charitynet.org

No responsibility for loss occasioned to any person acting or refraining from action as a result of the material in this publication can be accepted by the Charities Aid Foundation.

The publishers would like to thank Jo Habib of FunderFinder for her helpful comments and suggestions.

Contents

About the author 5

Introduction 6

CHAPTER ONE
Charitable trusts and what they fund 11
The older trusts 11
Trusts that fund innovative or 'unpopular' work 12
The smaller trusts 13
Different patterns of giving 14
Finding out about trusts 15

CHAPTER TWO
The competition 16
Assessing the competition 16
A typical trust's post bag 19

CHAPTER THREE
Sources of information on trusts 22
The Directory of Grant Making Trusts 22
A Guide to the Major Trusts 25
Other sources of information 26

CHAPTER FOUR
Selection of trusts 28
Affinity 28
Proximity 30

Size of grants made 31
How many trusts? 32

CHAPTER FIVE
What to do before drafting an application letter 33
Deciding how much to ask for 34
How to describe your organisation 35

CHAPTER SIX
The application 38
Presentation of your letter 38
What should your letter include? 40
What to enclose with your letter 41
Points to consider before sending off your application 42

CHAPTER SEVEN
How not to . . . 44

CHAPTER EIGHT
Following up your application 49
When no reply is received 49
When a negative reply is received 50
When a positive reply is received 51
Once a grant is made 52

CHAPTER NINE
Conclusion 55
Growing cooperation between trusts 55
Trusts are there to give money away 57

Useful organisations 58
Useful publications 60
About CAF 62
CAF publications 64
Index 70

About the author

Anne Villemur joined CAF in 1980 to help the then Editor to compile the 1981 edition of *The Directory of Grant Making Trusts*; in 1982 she became Editor herself.

Published every other year, the *DGMT* contains around 1,000 pages; updating it was a rather daunting task, compared by some to 'painting the Forth bridge'. Fortunately, most trusts were extremely cooperative in supplying new information to ensure the correctness of their entries.

Another enjoyable part of Anne's work was to organise, from 1983 onwards, workshops where groups of grant-seekers met with trust administrators to discuss how best to approach trusts.

Anne retired in November 1995.

Introduction

Grant-making charitable trusts and foundations often exist for the sole purpose of funding work carried out by charities and voluntary bodies. Funding work in a great many different areas, and free from political and commercial considerations, they represent a valuable source of independent funding for the voluntary sector.

What is a grant-making trust?

Grant-making trusts based in England and Wales are registered at the Charity Commission in the same way that grant-seeking charities are registered. Legally speaking, they are all 'charities'. Neither Scottish nor Northern Ireland trusts come under the Charity Commission; both are answerable to the Inland Revenue. The Scottish Charities Office, set up in 1992, investigates mismanagement or misconduct on the part of Scottish trusts.

At the origin of all trusts and foundations set up by a private person there is a settlor who, together with his/her chosen original trustees, decides on the aims and objectives – the charitable purposes – of the trust.

Charitable purposes are defined under four headings:
- the advancement of religion;
- the advancement of education;
- the relief of poverty;
- any other purpose beneficial to the community.

These will be set out in a trust deed, together with the amount of the trust's initial assets and the original trustees.

Many trusts decide to specify the widest possible aims and objectives, ie general charitable purposes. This makes it possible for them to fund a wide spectrum of charitable work without having to go through the process of altering the trust deed. The trust is then registered with the Charity Commission. The income generated by the assets will then become available for grant-making.

Three decades ago, trusts did little to publicise their activities. Today there are many sources, printed or otherwise, which describe their aims, grant-making procedures and financial position. Trusts have therefore become very much more visible; they have even been mentioned on BBC Radio 4's *The Archers* as a possible source of funds for a new village playground in Ambridge.

It is important to remember, however, that grant-making trusts are only one of several sources of funding for the voluntary sector. Although grant-aiding charitable work is their remit, the actual amounts of money involved should not be overestimated.

Charities will usually have to obtain support from a variety of funders – statutory sources, trusts and individuals (through local fundraising). Many of the bigger national trusts will expect to see local groups getting support locally before they consider providing funding themselves.

Other sources of funding for charitable work

The general public

From the humble collecting tin to deeds of covenant and legacies, the private donor has always been central to the support of charitable work. Dedicated individuals organise jumble sales, raffles, door-to-door collections, open days, etc, while volunteers of all ages participate in sponsored events and staff charity shops.

In recent years new means of giving have been introduced – for example the payroll giving scheme introduced in 1984 and Gift Aid, which allows for larger donations (minimum £250) to be made tax-effectively. It has been suggested that the impact of the National Lottery has been to reduce the amount of loose change finding its way into collecting tins and private individuals' response to charity mailshots but it is not at all clear from the evidence available so far that this is the case. What is clear is that the Lottery has served to make the work of charities more visible to the general public.

Corporate donors

A large slice of voluntary income is provided by companies. Unlike charitable trusts, companies, especially the larger ones, are very visible indeed – the proverbial household names. Their involvement, too, takes different forms: donations, gifts in kind, secondment of employees, sponsorship.

Naturally, there are sound commercial reasons for this involvement. Companies keep an eye fixed on the opinion of their customers and shareholders when choosing the type of work they wish to assist; they are also likely to keep their activities within the geographical area in which they trade.

Company giving is often of a practical nature: access to secretarial help, the printing of reports and brochures, and so on. At the higher end of the scale, large companies have often opted to set up their own charitable trusts, which operate independently of the parent body.

Statutory authorities

All officially elected bodies from parish councils to central government are empowered to make grants. In many areas, straight grants have now been superseded by contracts between the authorities and the service-providing charities.

Trust funding in perspective

The table below does not include all sources of income received by charities and voluntary bodies, but it does nevertheless demonstrate what a relatively small proportion of sector income is provided by trusts.

Some sources of voluntary sector income 1994–95

	£m
Central government (1993–94) (includes £2,955 million paid to voluntary housing associations)	3,567
Local authorities	1,271
Charitable trusts (Top 500)	704
Companies (Top 500) (includes charitable donations and other corporate support)	285
Individual giving (estimate for 1993)	5,300

CHAPTER ONE
Charitable trusts and what they fund

Trusts may be set up for a number of reasons. They are a tax-effective vehicle for philanthropy, largely because they do not pay tax on their income. They enable the person setting up the trust to give in perpetuity to their chosen cause. This chapter looks at the origins of charitable trusts and the different types of work that they fund.

The older trusts

The Directory of Grant Making Trusts lists 154 trusts which were set up before 1900. Among these, there are some whose assets are linked to what was, originally, purely local, parochial 'good works'. Some have assets that include property in large towns; these have greatly increased in size over the years.

The assets of many of the larger trusts stem from highly successful commercial ventures carried out by philanthropically minded families. Some of these trusts carry the name of the original settlor – Cadbury and Rowntree, for example – and still have members of the settlor's family on the Board of Trustees. The successful businessmen who set up these trusts had strong religious beliefs, which provided the motivation for philanthropy. Grant-making by these trusts at the end of the nineteenth century and the beginning of the twentieth tended to be based on a radical approach to the problems of the working class before the advent of the welfare state. This is exemplified in the Objects of the Carnegie United Kingdom Trust, which was established in 1913:

'Improvement of the well-being of the masses of the people of Great Britain and Ireland . . . and which the trustees select as best fitted from age to age for securing these purposes, remembering that new needs are constantly arising as the masses advance.'

Fortunes acquired through retailing in the postwar period have also been directed to charitable work, although here there has been a tendency to give a higher proportion to the arts and national heritage projects as opposed to concerns of a purely social nature.

Trusts that fund innovative or 'unpopular' work

Trusts which follow the radical, philanthropical approach to grant-making of the older trusts have been the source of funding for a large variety of innovative work of a 'social' nature. Trustees will tend to be interested in any project that fulfils a new need that has recently emerged. In addition, such trusts have often helped to set up projects dealing with so-called 'unpopular' causes (those most unlikely to attract donations from the general public or conservative-minded companies).

Trusts will also consider pilot schemes incorporating research into the causes of problems and possible remedial action in these new areas.

It used to be understood that these projects, once successful, would then receive funding from statutory bodies. This was known as **pump priming**; trusts were happy to go along with it as many of them considered that they were in the business of taking risks in order to achieve social progress.

In recent years, however, with large cutbacks in statutory funding, it has become less and less likely that projects which have got off the ground thanks to funding from trusts will receive money from local or central authorities. Understandably, trusts are most reluctant to step in where statutory funding has been withdrawn.

Where, then, lies the solution for the innovative project? Despite their dilemma – 'If we fund this project, how will it carry on when our grant has been used up?' – trusts do continue to grant-aid innovatory, experimental projects. They also continue to fund the so-called 'unpopular' causes. But inevitably it is more difficult to obtain funders.

A further solution for innovative (though not so much 'unpopular') projects lies with the general public – not through the collecting tin but through applying to appeals such as Telethon which fund a wide variety of work. The National Lottery Charities Board's first list of grants contained a number of small community-based organisations situated all over the United Kingdom.

The smaller trusts

There are also a great many smaller trusts. With limited resources, trustees will be naturally inclined to restrict their funding to one particular field of activity or one particular geographical area. This is usually the area where the trust is based, but the settlor or the trustees may also have a special interest in other places. This geographical bias can be most useful to community-based projects, where an invitation to visit the project to see what is being done can be issued to trustees and mutual cooperation built up.

Another bonus is that some local trusts remain virtually undiscovered; careful research may uncover extremely useful (if small) sources of funding. Unfortunately, it does not always follow that because a trust has remained hidden it is just waiting for your application: it may be just carrying on making donations to the settlor's favourite causes, year in, year out.

Different patterns of giving

It has been said that the strength of charitable trusts lies in their diversity. As long as they remain within the bounds of their trust deed, trustees are free to adopt patterns of giving which may differ widely from those of other trusts of similar size and origin.

Large or small grants?

Trusts may make a large number of small grants to voluntary bodies working in many different sectors; in this case they may not be concerned with following up the use to which the donation has been put – the sums involved may be too small to warrant such administration. Others may make a limited number of sizeable grants within areas determined by their current policy. In this case, the trustees will certainly require very careful investigations to be made before deciding whether or not to reply positively to an application and there will certainly be a follow-up procedure, most probably specified before the grant is made. Such grants may be made over two or three years, but most trusts are unwilling to tie up their funds for a longer period.

Proactive or reactive?

A small number of important trusts are proactive: they do not respond to applications as they arrive but instead decide on the work they wish to see succeed and search out organisations capable of carrying it out. They may well become involved in the management of the projects they fund.

Some trusts operate a mixture of these procedures, for example using the bulk of their income for proactive work but keeping a proportion for small grants to an established list of mainstream charities.

Finding out about trusts

There are some 180,000 charities on the Charity Commission Register. They are not divided into categories, for example grant-makers or grant-seekers, large or small. Charities working worldwide and local scout huts thus all appear on the same list. The Register presents an amorphous mass from which it is difficult to pluck the plums. Fortunately, there are many other ways of discovering which trusts are likely to be useful and what they are likely to fund. These sources of information are set out in Chapter 3.

CHAPTER TWO
The competition

In commercial business 'the competition' is represented by other companies producing similar lines in manufactured products or services. Such companies will be well aware of each other's existence.

For the grant-seeker, competition comes from just about any other charitable organisation which can apply for funding from trusts. It can also come from just about any part of the United Kingdom because a large proportion of trusts are set up to cover the whole country, although in practice they may centre on local projects within the towns or cities where they are based. Unless trusts have stated restrictions as to where the trustees prefer to make their grants, it is tempting to 'have a go' – wherever the trust is situated in relation to the grant-seeker.

Assessing the competition

National Lottery Charities Board list of grants

One excellent means of assessing the competition is to obtain the list of grants made by the National Lottery Charities Board. It is set out by region and shows the amount of money granted to projects and organisations.

Trusts' annual reports

Another means of discovering who else is working either in your particular field of activity or in your geographical area is to obtain the annual reports which are issued by the larger charitable trusts; these will list the beneficiaries of grants in the relevant financial year. In the case of the more open grant-makers, you will see not only to whom the grant was made and how much but also the exact purpose to which the funds were to be put. The more you can find out about the activities of trusts, the more likely you are to be successful.

The need to delve deeply

When trying to assess the competition, do not forget the role of the churches in community life. Most denominations now have halls and centres which are used for a wide variety of activities: mother and toddler groups, young people's clubs, fundraising meetings for overseas charities – as well as the work of the host church itself. If you see grants made to Saint X or Saint Y's, it may well be that these funds were destined for community work carried out on church premises.

It is also possible that the group involved was not itself a registered charity but was able to receive trust funds through the channel of the church, which does not itself need to be registered. Incidentally, not all trusts will fund unregistered bodies through the conduit of another organisation.

It is also worth remembering that some groups may have branched out and added other services to those for which they were originally set up. For example, a mother and toddler group may also provide a counselling service on childcare for single parents. Thus it can be seen that quite extensive delving is necessary to discover who is doing what and where.

In most places, useful sources of information are **Councils for Voluntary Service** and local authority **Voluntary Organisation Liaison Officers**, who will all provide not only lists of local voluntary bodies but also much other helpful information regarding the work of the voluntary sector. **Citizens Advice Bureaux** usually keep lists of voluntary organisations. Local newspapers, too, have sections on charitable events where you can see who is fundraising for what purpose.

The need for uniqueness

The necessity for groups, particularly new ones, to undertake this sort of research cannot be stressed too much. Many trusts complain that there is too much duplication, that groups are undertaking similar work within the same area without being aware of each other's existence.

It is only after assuring yourselves that the work you propose to do will indeed be unique to your area and thus merit funding from charitable trusts that you should start considering your application (or 'proposal' as some like to call it). If you discover that another group with the same aims as yourselves is working away in another part of your town, it might be better to consider joining forces with them.

CASE STUDY

In a country town in the south-east, a group of people who were already involved in running a club for local boys and girls under the aegis of their church became concerned when they came across an increasing number of seemingly homeless people, especially young ones, begging in the high street shopping centre. The more cautious members felt that they did not have the know-how to deal with the problem but were swept along by their more impetuous colleagues, who immediately set up a fundraising strategy for the provision of temporary accommodation in their town.

Fortunately, before any formal applications could be sent off to trusts, the Treasurer, who belonged to the more cautious wing of the club committee, made some enquiries among other church-based groups only to find that there was a very well run shelter in the next town down the railway line.

A typical trust's post bag

It can be helpful to put yourself in the position of the trust. Start by imagining a typical trust's post bag. It will be large and arrive daily, whatever the size of the trust itself. Remember that only the largest trusts will have paid staff to deal with the mountain of mail. Often the initial opening of envelopes is carried out by a solicitor's office. Many family trusts will depend on unpaid trustees to sift through the envelopes: large ones containing weighty brochures or annual reports; smaller window envelopes clearly produced by word processors; plain, handwritten envelopes which are curiously bulky (perhaps containing would-be students' CVs); flimsy airmail letters from Africa or the Indian subcontinent. How are you to ensure that your envelope will attract some attention among all the competition?

Mailshots from large charities

First, there will be mailshots from large charities – which are in fact far more likely to raise funds from the general public. However, some trusts do make grants to large organisations and inevitably have found their way on to mailing lists.

With these mailshots are usually enclosed hefty brochures or reports; these incur heavy postage costs and are in the opinion of many recipients a flagrant waste of charitable money. Nor does it help matters that mailing lists often include the same trust several times under a variety of slightly different names. The difference might lie in the administrator's name, or the title of the trust, or it might be as small as an extra comma (the database cannot be expected to tell the difference). The annoyance factor involved here means that the mailshot is not in serious competition with applications from projects and small groups, but they do add to the sorter's work.

Applications from students

Next, there will be the handwritten envelopes containing bulky CVs from people seeking educational grants in order to undertake second degrees or studies for which the relevant local authorities do not release funds. This category of application has increased greatly over recent years.

Why should so many individual people (as opposed to registered charities and voluntary bodies) believe that trusts will provide for them? It cannot be the fault of the published information available about trusts – some of which do fund individuals under certain circumstances: the majority definitely state that they are not empowered to make grants to individuals for any purpose. It is possible that people are advised to apply to trusts and supplied with a list of names and addresses without being told that any further research might be required.

Appeals from abroad

The same must apply to the often heartrending appeals from abroad, although the source of the lists provided to grant-seekers in this case is even more problematic. As with the mailshots from large organisations, these appeal letters do not constitute serious competition to good applications from small charities.

The real competition

The real competition will be from people like yourselves – those who are sensible enough to have asked themselves before applying 'Why should anyone give us money anyway?'

Among a pile of correspondence mainly destined for the bin, there will be lurking well-thought-out, precisely presented applications containing just enough backup material to allow trustees to evaluate exactly what the groups and organisations intend to do with the funds they seek. It is to be hoped that they will find their way on to the agenda of the next trustees' meeting. That is where they will come into competition with each other. Naturally, projects concerned with work dear to the hearts of the trustees will receive the most attention, but there is also hope for really new ideas and new ways of tackling old problems.

For reasons of confidentiality and time, trusts to which you have applied are unlikely to tell you what else is to be considered at any given meeting. Some projects may be proposing work with similar ultimate beneficiaries but the work itself may well be of a different type. That is why it is so important to research carefully, within your local area at least, to discover what is being undertaken by other voluntary organisations.

CHAPTER THREE
Sources of information on trusts

If you have been fundraising for some years, you will probably have built up a fairly comprehensive list of trusts most likely to fund your work. This will be invaluable and should be kept as up to date as possible, whether on card index or database.

For those who are new to approaching trusts, all available published information is an absolute must. Attendance at the seminars and workshops organised around the UK to promote better practice in grant-seeking is also extremely valuable.

The Directory of Grant Making Trusts

Finding out about charitable trusts is a very much easier proposition than it used to be. This is good news for the grant-seeker. It was not always like this. Prior to the publication of the first *Directory of Grant Making Trusts* (*DGMT*), charitable trusts and foundations enjoyed a degree of invisibility which now seems almost incredible.

It was in 1968 that the Charities Aid Fund (now the Charities Aid Foundation – CAF) published its first *DGMT*. It was based on the information on trusts contained in the official Register at the Charity Commission.

The Register itself had been set up following the 1960 Charities Act and was intended to be accessible to any member of the general public seeking information on the activities of a registered charitable body. The Register covered England and Wales and included all types of charity, whether grant-making or grant-seeking. As can be imagined, the sheer volume of the data involved did not make for easy reference.

CAF's aim in publishing the *DGMT* was to present details on the activities of trusts in a convenient book form; this would be especially helpful to small voluntary organisations that would have found it difficult to travel to London to consult the Register itself.

The original *DGMT* showed the stated objects of the trust listed and the type of work that had been funded but gave no information as to policy, restrictions, etc. This was remedied when the second edition appeared in 1971, as the compilers had decided to contact the trusts themselves, asking them to supply many more details than had been included in the first edition.

Classification of grants made

Another extremely important amendment was the decision to classify the actual grants made by the trusts. This is done following a system of identification which is unique to the *DGMT*. In practice, it entails all grants being classified by either the compilers or the trusts themselves identifying the nature of the work funded and attributing to it the relevant classification number.

CAF has published the *DGMT* every other year since 1971. The 1997–98 edition, split into two volumes for the first time and benefiting from a greatly improved classification system, contains details of almost 3,000 charitable trusts, showing what type of work they fund.

Using an up-to-date edition

There is one word of warning: do not use out-of-date editions. It is immediately obvious to trust officers and trustees that grant-seekers have not consulted the latest edition since addresses and even names of trusts change far more frequently than you might think. In any case, if trusts take the trouble to provide new information for their entries, with new lists of grants made or indications as to which areas the trustees are likely to fund, it is only sensible to make use of this new data.

If your group is not able to acquire its own up-to-date edition of the *DGMT*, your local reference library should be able to supply one (they could always get one in from another branch if they do not have it themselves). Councils for Voluntary Service (CVS) will have copies of the *DGMT* and of other publications concerning charitable trusts.

If you need to locate your local CVS, you should apply to the National Association of Councils for Voluntary Service (NACVS). In rural areas, information can be obtained from the relevant Rural Community Council. To discover your nearest one, you should get in touch with Action with Communities in Rural England (ACRE). Addresses are given at the back of the book. A list of all CVS in the UK is to be found in the annual *Charities Digest* published by the Family Welfare Association, 501–505 Kingsland Road, London E8 4AU.

The *DGMT Focus Series* and *Grantseeker*

A new CAF development is the *DGMT Focus Series*. This aims to collect together, in individual volumes, details of trusts which have expressed an intention to support charitable activity in particular fields. The first two to appear, *Children and Youth* and *Environment, Animal Welfare and Heritage*, focus on trusts supporting causes associated with these areas of work. Future titles, amongst others, will cover trusts that make grants for work overseas, offshore trusts which make grants into the UK and trusts that fund religious activities.

Two other titles in the series are the *Grants Index* and the *Trustees Index*. The former provides information on actual grants that leading trusts have made in the recent past. The latter lists all the trustees whose names are held on the *DGMT* database along with details of the trusts with which they are associated. Establishing 'who knows who' can be very useful for a fundraiser. Although attempts to 'nobble' trustees can backfire, privately most grant-seekers acknowledge that some of their biggest donations are received from trusts where a trustee is personally known to a member of their appeal committee.

Grantseeker is an interactive CD-ROM designed to scan the entire *DGMT* database and to provide users with a 'hit list' of trusts whose funding preferences accurately match their project or cause. See 'Useful publications' for details.

A Guide to the Major Trusts

Once publication of the *DGMT* had begun to open up the trust world and to allow easier public scrutiny of their activities, other publishing research organisations in the voluntary sector felt that they too could contribute to the dissemination of information useful to those looking for funding for charitable work. The less time people at the grass roots have to spend on raising funds, the more time they have for actually getting on with their real work. It was in 1987 that the Directory of Social Change produced their *Guide to the Major Trusts* (*GMT*).

To begin with, the *GMT* covered the 'top' 200 charitable trusts and foundations, but in quite a different way from the *DGMT*. The essential difference between the two books lies in the fact that in the *DGMT* any description of trustees' policy, type of grant made, etc, is supplied by the trusts themselves; if they do not cooperate (which is becoming rarer with each edition), the classification of the grants they have made serves as a guide to their activities. The *GMT*, on the other hand, does not classify grants made by trusts. When faced with lack of cooperation on the part of trusts, it will base the contents of individual trust entries on its researchers' extrapolation from the trust accounts contained in the relevant files on the Charity Commission Register. They comment on the lists of grants shown in the accounts, giving the names of recipients and the amounts of money involved.

The *GMT* is now published in two volumes covering 1,000 trusts. It is often advised that grant-seekers should use the *GMT* in conjunction with the *DGMT* to get as complete a picture as possible of trusts' grant-making.

CASE STUDY

One group involved in the upkeep of an ancient building had had the same Treasurer for a number of years (because no one would come forward to replace him). Although not exactly penny-pinching, this gentleman was certainly most penny-conscious. He resisted buying the new editions of the *DGMT* and *GMT* as and when published, to the point where many of the charity's applications were returned marked 'gone away'. One application was sent to the old address thrice removed of a certain itinerant trust. The trust had special forwarding arrangements but was not too impressed by a request for £10,000 from a charity that had obviously not acquired a new edition of the *DGMT* or *GMT* for years.

Other sources of information

Local guides

Apart from these two pioneering publications, there now exist a number of guides to local trusts produced by various organisations. However, they do not cover the UK in a homogeneous way. The Directory of Social Change (DSC) publishes guides for London, the Midlands, the North and the South. There are also guides produced locally for Merseyside, the North-East, Northern Ireland, Scotland and Wales. See 'Useful publications' for details.

The Charity Commission database

The Charity Commission itself has computerised the basic data contained in its charity Register; anyone can now consult the database at their offices in London, Taunton and Liverpool. Visitors to the Charity Commission can obtain information on trusts' title and objects and the correspondent's name and address. They can also obtain financial information if this has been supplied by the trust.

FunderFinder

One most interesting initiative taken in 1992 by the West Yorkshire Charities Information Bureau was the setting up of FunderFinder. FunderFinder is a national charity that produces computer software for grant-seekers. Its database, which is available on a subscription basis from its headquarters in Leeds (see 'Useful organisations'), is designed to help charities and voluntary organisations identify the charitable trusts which are most likely to help them.

The whole system is based on a classification of trusts' stated policies (not the grants they actually make), which was painstakingly evolved over a number of years. Charitable activity is described under three main headings: people, subjects and place. These in turn are broken down into a large number of subsections. Grant-seekers must classify their own work before using the resulting code to consult the database. Only titles of trusts are supplied, along with the relevant page numbers in the *DGMT* and the DSC guides.

Most Councils for Voluntary Service (CVS) subscribe to FunderFinder and allow voluntary organisations to consult the database. For details of how to locate your nearest CVS, see page 24.

A new venture is FunderFinder for Individuals, which is used by counselling organisations such as Citizens Advice Bureaux on behalf of individual clients.

Seminars and workshops

The seminars and workshops held around the UK to promote better practice in grant-seeking are another valuable source of information. These are run by the Directory of Social Change, the London Voluntary Services Council, Charities Aid Foundation and Charities Information Bureaux.

CHAPTER FOUR
Selection of trusts

There is no doubt about it, deciding which trust to apply to is time-consuming; to date, despite increasing computerisation, there is no short cut. For many years, people have been dreaming of being able to 'just press a button' and receive a printout of the trusts to which they should apply. However, until someone invents software that can mind-read or act as 'a fly on the wall' during trustees' meetings, it is much more likely that the combination of human intelligence and determination will succeed in reaching the desired result.

Given the very large number of trusts listed in the *DGMT* and *GMT*, how is it best to go about the task of selection without wasting your valuable time? What follow are some basic recommendations.

Affinity

The *DGMT* will, thanks to its classification system, show the type of work trusts have recently funded or intend to fund in the near future. The *GMT* will list the names of charities/groups which have received substantial grants. FunderFinder will present you with the names of trusts who, judging from their declared policies, might usefully be approached.

Defining your work

Before you can decide which trusts to approach, it will be necessary to define yourselves and your work. It is vital to try to do this from the viewpoint of an eventual funder. It is only natural to become so absorbed in your project that it seems that its main aim will be obvious to anyone. As discussed in Chapter 2, with so many often similar projects around, it is essential to be clear what is the main point about what you do and who are the ultimate beneficiaries.

This is a most important exercise. You must try to make sure that your objectives match what trusts say they will consider funding – not, of course, in an artificial way, twisting your objectives to fit trusts' declared policies, but in a positive way that takes into account who are the people who will benefit from your project.

Your project may, for instance, focus on helping elderly people to stay in their own homes for as long as possible. It may deal with all aspects of coping on your own: household gadgets, rearrangement of rooms and furniture, helplines, etc. You need money to train volunteers to become proficient in this area; they also need to learn to approach companies for gifts in kind, such as non-slip mats. It would be a mistake to label this 'education' – although it is, in a way. Look for trusts interested in elderly people and in carers.

Is your project an innovatory one?

Affinity can also be gauged from a much wider angle. If what you want to do (or are already doing) can be described as socially innovative, even 'political', then again trusts' declared interests in the *DGMT* and *GMT* should point you in the right direction. The restrictions and exclusions that are listed also give very helpful clues as to trustees' preferences.

If, on the other hand, your group provides a necessary but rather humdrum service to your local community, you would be better advised to look at more conservative-minded trusts whose trustees would baulk at funding anything of a risky nature.

Proximity

It is always a good idea to target trusts which are based locally to your own organisation. Not only will trustees have a much clearer perception of the value of your work – because they know the area – but it makes it easier for trust officers or trustees to visit you. There are several ways of finding out what your part of the country has to offer in the way of charitable trusts.

The *DGMT* has a geographical index that lists trusts according to their beneficial area, as stated in the main trust entry. A number of trusts are administered from the offices of solicitors or accountants; the official address may then be at variance with the stated beneficial area. The index lists trusts according to the geographical preferences of the trustees rather than the trust's official address.

When considering the question of proximity, a distinction should be made between large trusts with salaried staff and small and middling trusts which rely on the trustees themselves for their administration. Many of the latter, although originally set up to make grants nationally, will in practice confine themselves to giving locally or in areas known to the trustees, or they will perhaps remain faithful to the settlor's preferences. In some cases this can result in trusts listing beneficial areas which are geographically far apart. One trust in the *DGMT* had confined itself to West Sussex and Dumfries & Galloway.

Company trusts tend to confine their grant-making to the areas in which they operate commercially; this is good PR for them and a valuable source of funds for groups fortunate enough to work in these areas.

Community trusts and foundations

Another relatively recent source of local funding for those lucky enough to find themselves in the right area is community trusts and foundations. The idea for these was first introduced into the UK from the USA in 1986. Their remit is purely geographical but they do not cover all areas of the country. Their main characteristic is that they are both grant-seeking and grant-making since, with one or two exceptions, they had no substantial endowment at the outset. They are an extremely valuable asset to their local communities, and it is to be hoped that they will proliferate.

For a full list of community trusts and foundations, contact the Association of Community Trusts and Foundations (ACTAF); their address is at the back of the book.

Size of grants made

It is wise to approach trusts that usually give grants of the sort of size you are looking for. Thanks to the financial figures published in the *DGMT* and the *GMT*, it is easy to see the amount of money involved annually in trusts' grant-making.

Their total annual grant-making should not be the criterion used for selection, however. Some trusts, although relatively wealthy, tend to spread their largesse thinly over a very large number of organisations. Others make just a few sizeable grants within a carefully targeted area, although they may also have a programme of giving small grants for a particular type of work. Others do not appear to have any specific policy with regard to the size of grants made. Fortunately, entries in both the *DGMT* and the *GMT* give plenty of information on size of grants. Also, many trusts now produce annual reports which can be obtained on request.

It is always difficult to decide whether to apply for a large sum covering the whole cost of your project or to go for what could be described as 'a contribution' on the principle that every little helps. Sizeable, professionally administered trusts may be more likely to consider the former – 'contributions' often being considered to be in the domain of the public's generosity. This issue is discussed in more depth in Chapter 5. It is clearly not sensible to apply to very small trusts for amounts that would swallow up their entire annual income.

How many trusts?

Just how many trusts should be approached at any one time? There are two schools of thought, diametrically opposed to each other: the 'scatter-gun' approach versus careful targeting following painstaking research.

Careful targeting

Understandably, since they are on the receiving end of applications, trusts, when questioned on this subject, always insist on the necessity for voluntary organisations to adopt the path of careful targeting. This stance was summed up by the administrator of an important trust writing in the introductory section of the 1995 *DGMT*: 'It is a dreadful waste of time and money to "spray and pray", to scatter applications round dozens of trusts without checking whether they are up your street.' Many other trust officers have expressed this opinion, either in print or at the many meetings and seminars at which they speak.

The 'scatter-gun' approach

The opposite view, which is certainly not endorsed by trusts, can be summed up as 'If you don't ask, you won't get'. This engenders the deluge of inappropriate applications that cannot fail to waste everyone's time and money. The reasoning – if it can be called that – behind the latter stance seems to be that it is cheaper to use an unskilled volunteer to rattle off piles of blanket appeals from the word processor rather than to use the services of a member of staff to undertake a serious search, making use of the available information, and then produce properly thought-out applications.

CHAPTER FIVE

What to do before drafting an application letter

Only large 'household name' grant-seeking organisations have whole departments entirely given over to fundraising. Some of these departments are broken down into specialist areas with officers devoted to raising money from trusts as opposed to the general public, companies, etc. Lower down the scale, some charities can afford a single salaried fundraising officer who can devote his/her energies to this purpose alone. From a financial point of view this is an enviable position to be in. It must appear 'unfair' to smaller groups who do not dispose of these facilities.

When approaching charitable trusts, however, this seeming handicap may not be such a disadvantage as it seems. Trusts tend to be wary of anything that smacks of the slick and over-professional. This does not, however, mean that you should deliberately aim to appear as amateurish as possible. (It is tempting, of course, because the less time you have to spend on fundraising or grant-seeking, the more energy you can devote to the actual work in hand.) Although you do not need the slickness of some professional fundraisers, you do need to 'do your homework' and to appear well organised.

Some of this has already been covered. Chapter 2 discussed researching other organisations doing similar work to your own in the same geographical area and Chapter 4 looked at deciding which trusts to apply to. This chapter discusses deciding what type of grant to ask for – total funding for a project or a 'contribution' – and how best to present your case.

Deciding how much to ask for

The most important decision still to be made is what type of funding you are going to apply for.

Requests for 'a contribution'

Trusts do not usually see themselves as following the principle that 'every little helps' and would thus be unlikely to respond to a vague request for a 'contribution'. This may not, however, apply to smaller local trusts whose incomes are really too small to do anything but make a contribution and which are simply not geared to oversee in any detail the use to which their small grant has been put.

Obtaining core funding

The main hurdle facing most community-based voluntary groups is obtaining core funding; they cannot continue their work if they are constantly scratching around to pay the day-to-day expenses of heating and lighting, not to mention the salaries of paid workers. Unfortunately, most trusts are loath to provide core funding, especially in the present climate where it is highly improbable that statutory money will take over when the trust grant has been used up.

Funding for innovative projects

It is fortunate, in fact, that the trustees of large trusts do often prefer, if possible, to fund the truly innovative projects, as these might have great difficulty in getting off the ground if they had to rely on funds from any other source. Many trusts feel that they are in the business of making an impact on newly emerged problems. The guidelines of one of them states: 'Grants should have an impact, enabling something to happen which otherwise would not have been possible.'

Whole-project funding or the shopping list approach?

Whether your group has been nurturing an interesting piece of work for some time or you are proposing to set up something entirely new, when approaching the larger trusts your application may be more likely to attract their interest if your request is for funds to cover the whole project (where this is financially feasible) – though some trusts may be open to the possibility of partnership in funding.

When targeting medium-sized trusts (in terms of income), you obviously cannot expect funding to cover a whole project; in fact, it would be counter-productive to present your application in this way. What you can do is to select a part of the project which can, as it were, stand alone and so offer the trustees the possibility of making their mark on the project.

This preference for making an impact, however small, on charitable projects could be catered for by adopting a type of application known as the 'shopping list'. It consists in setting out a list of items required for the work, showing their estimated cost and inviting trusts to choose what they would like to provide. This type of approach may appeal to some trusts but not others.

How to describe your organisation

Another piece of 'homework', which applicants do not always seem to undertake before drafting a letter of application, is to arrive at a very clear description of your organisation, which will allow the reader to understand, more or less at a glance, what your project is all about. It is quite astonishing the number of grant-seekers who suppose that trust officers are in some way clairvoyant and do not require all the details about the applicant organisation or that their patience is limitless and that they will be only too pleased to extract the essential information from pages of vague waffle.

CASE STUDY

A small community group in Liverpool was aiming to provide counselling and advice, especially on welfare rights, to black people and other ethnic minorities within their part of the city. There was much discussion within the group as to how to describe themselves when drafting their application letter to trusts. Some group members were anxious to avoid the word 'black' or even 'ethnic minority'. Had the more down-to-earth members fallen in with their wishes, the resulting letter would have been so convoluted that the most sympathetic administrator would have given up trying to understand it.

Fortunately, those in favour of plain English prevailed as they were able to point out that several important trusts regularly used the 'offending' words themselves in their entries.

What trusts need to know, as succinctly as possible, is as follows:

Who you are

The title of your organisation may state this clearly but most probably it does not. You need to highlight, as early as possible in your letter of application, the ultimate beneficiaries of your work. It should also contain a description of the group itself: its size, when it was set up, the ratio of salaried workers to unpaid volunteers.

What you do

Suppose that you are concerned with homelessness – a vast area which, most unfortunately, is becoming more vast. There are large national charities concerned with homelessness. It is important that your committee should decide what part of this area your work covers since it is impossible for small groups to do more than help within a restricted area.

If, for example, you provide counselling, it is useful to measure your work in terms of number of 'clients' and number of hours spent with them.

Why you do it

This will call for in-depth discussion on the part of the committee. The newer the project, the easier this will be. Longer-established projects may have to return to their grass roots to discover the reason for the original spark which caused the establishment of the project.

Where you do it

Unless you are applying to local trusts, it will be necessary to define the territory within which you work; especially in a large urban area, it is important to show clearly where you work. Trusts cannot be expected to have exact prior knowledge of your locality.

When you want to do it

It is absolutely essential that your group should define clearly what future objectives you have, bearing in mind that trust grant-making is generally not instantaneous. Most trusts meet only three or four times a year and some have a waiting list; this means that an application can be held pending for as much as six months before it is put before a trustees' meeting. If the funds you require are needed for the day after tomorrow, trusts will usually not be able to help – though they do sometimes respond immediately to individuals and in emergencies.

How much is required

This is the item which should provoke the most discussion before the application is drafted. Trustees will want to know in some detail the amount of money required to fund the work you are proposing to undertake. Many trustees are professional accountants; they will certainly want to see a precise and realistic budget. It is a surprising fact that many an otherwise well-presented application carries no mention of the amount of money required. If any of the above information is not included, your application will not attract the attention it deserves.

CHAPTER SIX
The application

Time spent on the research and preparation outlined in the previous chapters is never wasted, although busy committee members may feel that it is interfering with the 'real' work of the group. It would be a waste of time, however, if all this effort did not result in the sort of application which stands out among all the others for its clarity and interest.

This is not such a tall order as it sounds. Grant-seekers should try to put themselves in the place of the person on the receiving end of the application rather than adopt what might be described as the 'message in a bottle' mode, which seems to stem from uncertainty as to whether there is any one 'out there' who will come to the rescue.

Presentation of your letter

Your letter head

Your first contact with the trusts you have chosen should leave no doubt as to your group's identity. From a practical point of view, this will mean a clear, uncluttered letter heading on which the title of your organisation is the main item to meet the eye. Too many groups try to illustrate their objectives by the use of amateur drawings. These tend to raise queries about their aims rather than the reverse.

If it is important to show clearly the identity of your group on the letter heading, it is also useful to co-opt well-known members of the 'great and good' to become patrons of your organisation. Their names printed at the foot of your paper will certainly lend credibility, especially if the people concerned are recognised to have a strong interest in the problem you are addressing.

The last thing that an application to a trust should resemble is a circular 'mailshot' letter. This can cause problems.

CASE STUDY

In Wiltshire, some narrowboat enthusiasts had devised a scheme to offer days out on the canal to disabled people. Their original motivation had been to restore the canal itself; the idea of helping disabled people stemmed from one of the members who worked as a volunteer with a disability charity.

For the conservation work on the canal the general public had been the main benefactors; now they were going to apply to trusts. Two decisions regarding the application letter to address to trusts had to be taken: (a) Should they employ a professional fundraiser as none of them had much experience of trusts? (b) Could they use the attractive headed paper illustrating the narrowboat without it being instantly binned as a circular mailshot? In the end they decided to draft their own letter but they splashed out on a more sober letter heading. Their strategy proved successful.

Using a computer or word processor

It is not such a long time ago that the word processor was not in almost universal use. At that time, grant-seekers were anxiously asking if word-processed applications were acceptable. One memorable reply from a trust officer was: 'Well, you could add a touch of Tipp-Ex just to personalise it . . .'

It may now seem slightly ludicrous that anyone should ever have felt that word-processed application letters were in any way unacceptable, but it should be remembered that it was the word processor which unleashed the deluge of mainly inappropriate applications to trusts.

The trouble with word processors is that, unlike individually typed letters, they allow for the churning out of letters with minimal alterations as to name, address, etc. The most common complaint made by trusts is that they receive applications that are addressed to them but mention another trust's name in the body of the letter. Although it is cost-effective as far as secretarial expense is concerned, addressing the same letter to a wide variety of trusts is not the best way of approaching charitable trusts. Not that you should bend your project to fit the policy of the trust you are writing to: this would probably be noticed and noted against you. However, each trust does have its own distinct identity and it is only sensible to take this into account when drafting your letter.

How long should the letter be?

Naturally you should be as concise as possible without leaving out essential information. The consensus among trust officers would seem to be that two sides of A4 should suffice to put your case. Once again, try to put yourself in the place of the person faced with a pile of applications on a wet Monday morning. After all, it is the trust officer who has to present them in précis form to the trustees. No wonder that one of them stated a preference for the 'short and snappy'.

What should your letter include?

Whatever you achieve in shortness and snappiness, your letter must include the following essential points:

The potential beneficiaries Who exactly are the people who will benefit – in terms of age group, ethnicity, gender, medical condition? The more precisely you can draw a pen portrait of your 'clients', the more helpful it will be to the recipient of your application.

The perceived need Is the work you propose to undertake really necessary? If it is truly innovative, you will already have a very good idea of its value. If it is of a more humdrum nature, you will need to stress the new thinking that you have brought to tackle the problem.

The absence of others working in the field Are you quite sure that no one else has already started up a similar project within your geographical area? Trusts will want to make sure that they do not fund duplicated work.

Proof that the work will make a real difference Have you a really clear idea of what you will achieve? Do not be pessimistic on this point. If you have got this far in planning your project, you must be convinced of its usefulness. A tone of quiet confidence will help to advance your case.

Monitoring and evaluation How do you propose to check on the progress of your work and to assess its overall usefulness and effectiveness?

What to enclose with your letter

You will not want to produce a huge missive likely to discourage even the most dedicated of trust officers, but there are some items which are absolutely essential:

- a detailed budget for the project or part of the project for which you are applying;
- an up-to-date set of the organisation's audited accounts;
- a copy of your most recent annual report;
- should your project concern a building, plans for the building.

The third item has often been the object of discussion. If your annual report – a legal requirement and an essential enclosure – takes the form of a 'glossy brochure', will this be offputting to trusts, suggesting as it may do that the organisation it describes is spendthrift?

Some trusts will be put off, but others will not. One way round the dilemma is to try to get your annual report or other brochure (perhaps relating to a particular appeal) sponsored by a company and make sure that the sponsorship is prominently displayed.

But it is not always the contents of the envelopes sent by grant-seekers that lead their recipients to accuse them of extravagance. High postage costs are often considered to be a waste of charitable money. One trust administrator was prompted to devise a 'Ready Waste Reckoner' showing the very high cost of sending (and replying to) ill-directed applications.

Lastly, if you do have a video of your work, do not be tempted to send it to a trust; it will not be watched (lack of time), and in any case all material you send will most probably have to be condensed by the trust officer before it is put to the trustees.

Points to consider before sending off your application

Have you used the most up-to-date editions of the *DGMT* and *GMT*? Nothing is more likely to consign your application to the wastepaper basket than to use the name of a retired administrator, a trust title that has been changed or a previous address. As one trust administrator (female) remarked, 'I do prefer not to be addressed as Dear Sir'. You might feel that in the 1990s such niceties are no longer of any importance. Despite this, remember that you hope that your application will receive due attention – any attention to detail on your part can only be of benefit.

Has the letter been signed and by whom? It may seem incredible but otherwise well-presented applications do arrive at their destination unsigned. Also, it is necessary to make sure that the signatory is the most important officer of your organisation and not just whoever happens to be available when the letter is ready to be signed. Should you decide to ask a prestigious patron to sign the letter, go over it for spelling. Lord X or Baroness Y will probably sign it without noticing that you cannot spell 'catalyst'.

Have you checked the English? If English is the second language of your group, incorrect English should not be a drawback when applying to large proactive trusts, but it can be a problem when contacting smaller trusts which do not have staff. Before writing the letter, it would be sensible to get outside help with the actual wording.

Should you telephone the trust before writing to enquire whether or not it would be worthwhile to send a formal application? Some trusts definitely prefer an initial telephone call, as this serves to cut down on correspondence. You can discover which ones are in this category by consulting their entries in the *DGMT* – those which supply telephone numbers should not mind being called.

Does the trust issue printed guidelines for applicants? If it does, it is only sensible to get hold of these before sending an application. Again, entries in the *DGMT* should mention that guidelines are issued. Other trusts may insist on the use of their official application form; this, too, should be noted in their entries in the *DGMT*. When in doubt, and only if a telephone number is shown, you could call them to ask if they have an application form.

Should you suggest in your letter that trust officers visit your organisation? Some trusts always visit, others never. It really comes back to the question of whether or not there are enough staff. It is probably not worth proposing a visit: if a trust is in the habit of visiting, then it will. If you do prefer to invite a visit, make sure that you are being realistic as regards the distance to be travelled.

Should mention be made of other trusts approached and the result? Most definitely yes for those with whom you have been successful or who have shown a definite interest in your project. It is not necessary to list trusts who have 'regretted that the trustees . . .' or who have not replied at all. Reporting success with others can only be helpful. If you are entirely new to approaching trusts this should be made clear, not forgetting that trusts do seek out innovation.

CHAPTER SEVEN

How not to...

Around the beginning of the 1980s, various organisations in the voluntary sector, of which CAF was one, decided that there should be more openness between grant-makers and grant-seekers. Charity conferences, seminars and workshops were organised for delegates from charities and voluntary groups, large and small, where they could come and listen to trust administrators and company grant-makers and question them on their policies and restrictions. Not surprisingly, these meetings were very popular with grant-seekers.

One series of workshops was started in 1983 by CAF. The main outcome of the workshops was positive advice on how best to approach charitable trusts, but there were also very useful tips on 'How not to do it'. Some of the points mentioned by the trust speakers may seem almost too obvious to be noted, but some groups somewhere must have made the errors which came to the trusts' notice. This chapter summarises some of the points that were raised.

Workshops on raising money from trusts are now held regularly throughout the UK. For more information see page 27.

Compliance with trusts' procedures

Do not ignore trusts' guidelines. Some trusts use official application forms which are designed to simplify administration and make it easier to present the applications to trustees. They may seem bureaucratic and difficult to fill in, but if that is what is required, the effort will have to be made. The same applies to deadlines for submissions: whatever problems may have caused your delay, you must try to surmount them so as not to miss the boat.

Timing of your application

Do not ask for money for help in a crisis. Although trust staff or the hard-pressed volunteer secretaries will be sifting and preparing applications throughout the year, trustees' meetings are usually held only three or four times a year. It is for future finance that trusts should be approached; they can very rarely be of help in a crisis such as the one which happened to an equine sanctuary under threat of eviction from council land. The sanctuary management waited until the very last moment, hoping for a reprieve which did not come, then began frantically telephoning trusts. They could not, of course, be of help at such short notice.

Presentation

Do not send a handwritten letter, however clear your writing. It may seem unfair, especially in the case of small groups struggling to get off the ground, but no one expects to have to decipher handwriting as part of their work. Finding a volunteer to type or word-process is really essential.

At the other end of the presentation scale, a slick duplicated mailshot is almost certain to end up in the wastepaper bin. Such material is really suitable for use only when approaching the general public for donations.

Bad English

Do not send a letter containing bad grammar and wrong spellings. It has already been mentioned that if English is not the first language of the group, trusts will generally understand and make allowances, but it is still better to seek help.

Allowances are unlikely to be made for those who should be able to write correct English. We may no longer be in the era of trust administrators bristling at split infinitives but applications should not contain spelling mistakes or really shaky grammar.

Jargon and 'political correctness'

Do not expect trusts to understand the jargon you use in your daily work. They may be irritated, too, by an excess of political correctness, without going to the lengths of one trust which states in its *DGMT* entry: 'The trustees will use their best endeavours not to be prejudiced against an application that uses the jargon evolved by the new Welfare Industry such as caring, under-privileged and deprived.'

An over-confident approach

Do not use an approach with trusts just because it has been successful elsewhere. They may require different treatment. You may, for example, have made some headway with local dignitaries who support your work and have written glowing testimonials in its favour. You may well find these useful in applying to the public for money, but beware of this approach when dealing with trusts: it can easily backfire by making you seem so self-sufficient that trust money would be wasted on you.

An under-confident approach

Do not appear lacking in confidence. If too much confidence can be a mistake, so can too little. Never threaten that valuable work will have to cease if the trust applied to does not come up with a grant because the group's finances are at rock bottom. This will not encourage trustees to make what they will perceive to be a most ill-advised investment.

'Bending' your aims to suit the trust

Do not attempt to 'bend' the aims of your organisation to suit the trust you are applying to. The trust administrator is a wily bird. Practice makes perfect; reading applications and extracting the essential from the padding is what an administrator's job is all about. Any manipulation of a group's aims and objectives to fit the trust's stated policy is therefore likely to be pounced upon immediately and will effectively put paid to the applicant's hopes of creating a relationship with that particular trust.

What would be acceptable is to hive off, where possible, the part of your project which does have a chance of being put before a trustees' meeting. If, for example, you are proposing to renovate a community centre in an inner city and one of the trusts you have selected is resolutely against funding bricks and mortar, an application to fund a computerised system for learning English as a second language might nevertheless succeed.

Implying that people cannot make up their own minds

Do not say anything to imply that the person reading the application is not capable of making up his or her own mind. Ending an application letter by expressing the hope that 'this application will be taken seriously' may constitute a serious error.

Emotive language

Do not use excessively emotive language. 'Gush' is how one trust director described the style of applications which are low on facts but high on emotion.

It is true that small groups working at grass-roots level need all the enthusiasm that they can muster if they are to succeed. It is also easy to imagine that your project and its beneficiaries are of such supreme importance that grant-makers will queue up to fund it. The fact is that trusts are in a position to have seen large numbers of the same type of worthy project from all around the UK.

Extravagant claims

Do not make extravagant claims. The claim that one grant to a very small organisation will allow for the immediate eradication of a nationwide problem such as the break-up of families is not likely to sound very credible.

Nor is it a good idea to describe a project involving access for the disabled to a church loo as 'unique and exciting'. Access to and within any public building is certainly extremely important, and schemes to provide access have for some years been funded by a number of trusts, but they can hardly be described as 'new' or 'unique'.

CASE STUDY

Trust administrators have a unique perspective on social needs because of the multitude of applications they receive. A community group in Bristol had not realised this fact – perhaps they still held on to a perception of trusts as being out of touch with everyday life. Their application for funding to enable them to add extra kitchen facilities to their drop-in centre for young unemployed people was couched in glowing terms suggesting that a grant to this small organisation would more or less eradicate the problem of unemployment nationwide.

Evidence of such blinkered self-satisfaction was not likely to impress trust officers, who had been funding drop-in centres all over the UK for many years. A more realistic approach would certainly have helped.

Errors that could easily be avoided

Some mistakes are very easily avoided, however small and overworked the group may be. The most embarrassing must be the duplication of applications. To send your application twice within a few days to the same trust seems unbelievable but it does occur; a simple card index system will suffice to prevent this happening. Sending out-of-date supporting material with your application may save a little money but it will not help your approach to trusts.

CHAPTER EIGHT

Following up your application

There must be a feeling of relief, of a job well done, when at last a batch (it is to be hoped small) of applications has been posted out. This happy feeling can turn to anxiety when the expected rapid response does not materialise. Given the competition and all the possible pitfalls into which you can fall when presenting your project to trusts, it is only too easy for the grant-seeker to feel that the application will not succeed and that you might as well forget all about it.

Remember that trusts are not geared to give instant replies; there are no quick answers. When approaching trusts, it is a question of thinking and planning in months rather than weeks.

Let us consider what should be done in the event of the three possible results to your approach:

- no reply
- a negative reply
- a positive reply

When no reply is received

This is always rather bewildering. What is the timescale involved in 'no reply'? Should a reply of any sort be expected at all? How long should you wait before making discreet enquiries?

Clues are to be found in the entries in the *DGMT*. Some of the more helpful ones will clearly state whether or not applicants can expect an answer and under what circumstances. A number of major trusts used always to reply to every application (except the mailshot variety), if only by a standard postcard of rejection. Unfortunately, the rising tide of applications has obliged some of them to give up automatic replies because of the sheer cost; this fact should be noted in their entries.

Some trustees, who evidently wish to avoid all contact with applicants, state tersely: 'No response will be made to unsolicited applications.' This is clearly a smokescreen. Although it implies that the trustees are busy proactively seeking out worthy causes, you have only to research the grants they have actually made to realise that this is most unlikely. It is not worth waiting for their reply.

Telephoning to see what has happened

With the friendlier trusts, should you telephone to see what has happened? Look at their entries in the *DGMT* again: if there is a telephone number included in the entry, this should mean that they are not against contact being made in this way.

Grant-seekers following up an application should look at the relevant entry in the *DGMT* to see if the dates of trustees' meetings are shown. Where none are shown, you should wait around six weeks.

Any form of follow-up after the initial application will require you to keep a very careful record of all applications to and contact with trusts. Ideally this should be computerised, but any type of written record is better than none. It will also be of great help to your group if there are changes in its management.

When a negative reply is received

Any answer is presumably better than none. At least you know where you stand vis-à-vis this particular trust. Or do you?

Some trusts have resolutely adopted the principle of replying only to prospective grantees, others have various means of rejecting applications.

- Some will send a curt postcard of rejection with no explanation as to the reason. This leaves you in almost the same position as if there had been no response at all. If you can glean no clue from the entries in the *DGMT* and the *GMT*, you could perhaps wait a year or so and try again.
- Some have standard rejection letters which include a reason for their negative reply. Should this letter state that your work is not within their guidelines, then you have probably made a mistake in interpreting their stated policy (or maybe the policy has recently been changed). You could perhaps query this decision if you feel that there has been a misunderstanding.
- Another kind of negative letter will state that 'the trustees regret that their funds are fully committed'. Some add 'for the foreseeable future'. In the first case this may warrant you applying again at a later date; in the second it is unlikely to be worth persevering.

Any rather vague letter of rejection which seems to leave a faint ray of hope for the future is certainly worth 'putting on the back burner'.

However infuriated you may feel when you are rejected by a trust whose policy you had felt fitted exactly with the work of your project, do not give in to the temptation to write back to voice a protest. Trustees change, as do their policies; you may succeed in the future but not if a furious or rude letter from your group is on their files.

When a positive reply is received

Following on from so many considerations on the difficult task of selecting trusts, the fact that they are currently inundated with applications, the many things one should do and not do and how to deal with rejection, the thought of actually receiving a grant seems to have receded beyond the horizon . . .

Requests for further information

A positive reply may not take the form of a definite offer of a grant. You must be ready for almost any eventuality.

- If you have applied for a substantial sum, trusts may well require further information. Make sure that you have it to hand so that you can supply it straight away.
- They may want to make a visit before the next trustees' meeting. Will your committee be available?
- Will you be able to answer awkward questions as to whether you think that your innovatory work is possible to replicate elsewhere?
- Have you set aside some funds in order to monitor the project once it is up and running?

Trustees may want you to answer certain questions before they make a grant. You need to be able to supply the response to any query without delay.

Once a grant is made

Once a grant is made, there is an agenda for follow-up which will enable you to establish an ongoing relationship with the trusts. Here again, some of the advice may seem ludicrously elementary, but it does stem from errors which have actually been noted by trust administrators.

Acknowledging letters and cheques

Astonishingly, some letters enclosing cheques are not acknowledged nor are any thanks addressed to the trustees. It is only when the cheque appears on a bank statement that there is any confirmation that it actually arrived at its destination. Whatever the reason for this apparent churlishness, any further approach by the group in question is unlikely to succeed.

Keeping the donor informed

It is not only elementary politeness that is required; some grants may be accompanied by specific requests as to, for example, the timing of the work to be carried out. As far as possible, try to comply with these requirements and keep the donor trust informed. Whether the grant comes with strings attached or not, you will probably want to reapply at some later date and ideally create a cooperative relationship – particularly with the larger trusts, who often like to see their grant-making as a partnership rather than a hierarchical relationship between donor and recipient.

Proactive or not, trusts will want to know what has happened to their grant. It is a good idea to send them progress reports and to let them know whether you have actually reached your target or not. After all, if the trustees had enough interest in your project to make a grant, they will certainly want to know how it is getting on.

For small, no-strings-attached grants, a copy of the following annual report, probably including a list of grants received, would be sufficient in the way of follow-up.

Inviting trustees or trust administrators to visit

If no one from the trust visited before the grant was made, you might usefully invite the administrator or a trustee to come along to see how things are shaping up. They may be too busy, but if they do respond to your invitation make sure that they can meet the people you are helping in a friendly, relaxed way. Too often trust visitors are treated like dignitaries to be swept past the 'customers' into some inner sanctum where management has set out a dainty tea.

Monitoring and evaluation

Another form of follow-up came to the fore in the 1980s when everyone was being urged to be more businesslike. It is the system of monitoring and evaluation. In this context, 'monitoring' means any form of checking by a trust that a grant awarded to an organisation is being or has been properly spent. 'Evaluation' means assessing what impact the grant has had on the problem being addressed.

Monitoring and evaluation cost money. Many trusts, both with and without paid staff, monitor even small, one-off grants. If, for example, a grant is made to an individual to buy furniture, a receipt is often required. Evaluation is carried out by very few trusts, regardless of size.

Given that monitoring and evaluation have become something of a 'flavour of the month', particularly with the more progressive trusts, it could be helpful if your initial approach incorporated some mention of the process and how you feel it could be carried out. In fact, whatever you can do to show that you are knowledgeable about trustees' aims and aspirations rather than seeing them as a sort of bank, the more likely you are to succeed in your grant-seeking.

CHAPTER NINE
Conclusion

So much advice on what not to do and how to do things in an acceptable way may give the impression that approaching trusts is a hopeless task. This gloomy picture is entirely false.

While there are rules to be observed, it is vital to remember that, as one trust officer remarked, grant-makers and grant-seekers are 'on the same side': both are there to advance the invaluable work of the voluntary sector.

The most crucial thing for grant-seekers is to understand that trusts' stated policies and restrictions really are an accurate description of what they will and will not do. People should not act on the assumption that 'they are all worth a try' – as though approaching trusts were some sort of game or lottery.

The vast majority of trusts now agree that openness can only be of benefit to people on either side of the fence. This has resulted in their being more forthcoming when the compilers of directories and guides apply to them for guidelines and up-to-date information.

Growing cooperation between trusts

Some time ago, they also began to recognise the value of an interchange of ideas and a sharing of experiences between trust directors and administrators. The first step in this direction was the Foundation Forum, a club-like get-together of a dozen or so directors of very large trusts. Then, in the early 1980s, a group of assistant directors met for a short study seminar. This was so successful that it was decided to make it an annual event. The new organisation was called the Charitable Trusts Administration Group. A number of interest groups were also formed by trusts which had common grant-making programmes. These included Neighbourhood Issues, Northern Ireland, Penal Affairs, Race Relations and Women's Issues.

The Association of Charitable Foundations

As the activity of the Group expanded, many administrators felt that a more formal association of trusts should be formed, including both trustees and administrators. Thus, in 1989, the Association of Charitable Foundations (ACF) came into being, with the following aims and objectives:

'To support the work of charitable trusts and foundations by: establishing common ground from which members can speak to government, local authorities and the business and voluntary sectors; seeking to improve the public's understanding of what trusts and foundations can and cannot do; enabling trusts and foundations to learn from each other's experience and good practice; encouraging the formation of new grant-making foundations.'

ACF now has a membership of 234 trusts and foundations, some very large, some quite small; the interest groups address 20 different subjects. A seminar programme to promote good practice is an important part of its work. ACF also produces publications, the latest of which, published in 1995, has a title which should hearten all grant-seekers. It is called *Fairness in Funding*.

Further experiments in cooperation

The very fact of trusts associating seems to have created a momentum towards innovation. In the north-east of England, a group of trusts has been meeting regularly to exchange views on local funding, a sort of mini ACF. Recently they decided to create a database on which were to be logged the applications they received together with details of the projects and the decision of the trustees as to whether they should be funded. This data is made available only to grant-makers in the north-east. The trust administrators involved have found that this enables them to present a more balanced view of applications to their trustees. Like all good ideas, this one is likely to spread to other parts of the UK grant-making scene.

Trusts are there to give money away

There are some grant-seekers who view all this cooperation and exchange of information between trusts with some alarm: people are afraid that their organisation might be blackballed as a result. When this question is raised at workshops or seminars, these fears are always allayed by trust speakers, who insist that the cooperation is only in the interest of trust officers and trustees and does not in any way imply that positive or negative decisions are taken mutually.

It is all too easy to imagine that trusts are unfriendly and judgemental, warding off the grant-seeker with the well-worn phrase 'funds fully committed for the foreseeable future'. There are trusts who use these words as a smokescreen but there are a great many for whom the words are true because they are engaged in some particular long-term project. They would like to help if they could.

Trust administrators are also very knowledgeable about what is going on in the voluntary sector; it may be worth contacting them for advice even if they are not in a position to make a grant.

It cannot be repeated too often: trusts are in the business of giving money away. As one trust director remarked (in two languages): 'Do not despair – *Nil desperandum!*'

Useful organisations

Action with Communities in Rural England (ACRE)
Umbrella organisation for Rural Community Councils.

Somerford Court
Somerford Road
Cirencester
Glos GS7 1TW
Tel 01285 653477

Association of Charitable Foundations (ACF)
Organisation to promote the effectiveness of UK grant-making trusts.

4 Bloomsbury Square
London WC1A 2RL
Tel 0171-404 1338

Association of Community Trusts and Foundations (ACTAF)
Umbrella organisation to which all community trusts and foundations belong.

4 Bloomsbury Square
London WC1A 2RL
Tel 0171-831 0033

Charity Commission

St Alban's House	2nd Floor	Woodfield House
57–60 Haymarket	20 Kings Parade	Tangier
London SW1Y 4QX	Queens Dock	Taunton
Tel 0171-210 4556	Liverpool L3 4DQ	Somerset TA1 4BL
	Tel 0151-703 1500	*Tel* 01823 345000

Information about charitable trusts can be viewed on screen at the Central Register in the three locations above. The paper files on these trusts containing full financial accounts can be seen but must be requested in advance of your visit. Photocopies of parts of these accounts are provided to visitors for a small fee.

Directory of Social Change (DSC)

24 Stephenson Way
London NW1 2DP
Tel 0171-209 4949

An educational charity which publishes a wide variety of books designed to help charities to raise funds from a number of sources including charitable trusts, companies and local funders. The DSC also runs workshops and seminars throughout the UK on raising funds for charitable work.

FunderFinder
Produces computer software for grant-seekers that is designed to help them identify the trusts most likely to help them.

65 Raglan Road
Leeds LS2 9DZ
Tel 0113 243 3008

London Voluntary Service Council
Runs seminars and workshops and publishes a magazine called Voluntary Voice *which appears ten times a year.*

356 Holloway Road
London N7 6PA
Tel 0171-700 8107

National Association of Councils for Voluntary Service (NACVS)
Umbrella organisation for local Councils for Voluntary Service (CVS).

3rd Floor
Arundel Court
177 Arundel Street
Sheffield S1 2NU
Tel 0114 278 6636

National Council for Voluntary Organisations (NCVO)
An umbrella body offering help and advice (especially legal advice) to all charitable organisations.

Regent's Wharf
8 All Saints Street
London N1 9RL
Tel 0171-713 6161

Scottish Council for Voluntary Organisations (SCVO)
The Scottish equivalent of the NCVO.

18–19 Claremont Crescent
Edinburgh EH7 4QD
Tel 0131-556 3882

Useful publications

CAF publications

The Directory of Grant Making Trusts Published every other year. 15th edition 1997–98, 2 volumes. £69.95. Covers around 3,000 charitable trusts cross-referenced under hundreds of fields of charitable interest they support.

The DGMT Focus Series includes the following titles:

Children and Youth (1996) £19.95. Focuses on trusts supporting causes in this area of work.

Environment, Animal Welfare and Heritage (1996) £19.95. Focuses on trusts supporting causes in these areas.

Grants Index (1997) £14.95. Provides information on actual grants made by leading trusts in the recent past.

Trustees Index (1997) £14.95. Lists all trustees whose names are held on the *DGMT* database along with details of the trusts with which they are associated.

Grantseeker (1997) £176.25 incl. VAT. An interactive CD-ROM designed to scan the entire *DGMT* database and to provide users with a 'hit list' of trusts whose funding preferences match their project or cause.

See also pages 64–69.

DSC publications

A Guide to the Major Trusts, Vol 1 Published every other year. 5th edition 1995–96. £15.95. Covers 300 trusts that make grants of over £200,000 a year. Gives examples of the actual grants they have made.

A Guide to the Major Trusts, Vol 2 Published every other year. 2nd edition 1995–96. £15.95. Covers 700 trusts that make grants of at least £45,000 a year.

The DSC also publishes guides to local trusts in the following areas, all priced £13.95:

1 *North* **2** *Midlands*
3 *London* **4** *South*

Other publications

The Directory of Scottish Grant-Making Trusts SCVO. £12.50.

Fairness in Funding: An equal opportunities guide for grant-makers (1995) Published by the Association of Charitable Foundations, 4 Bloomsbury Square, London WC1A 2RL. £7. Gives an insight into current debates among grant-makers. Also contains a reading list.

Funding for Voluntary Action Free from Northern Ireland Voluntary Trust, 22 Mount Charles, Belfast BT7 1NZ.

Merseyside Directory of Grant-Making Trusts From Communications Dept, Liverpool CVS, 14 Castle Street, Liverpool L2 0NJ. £6.95.

North-East Guide for Grant Seekers Funding Information North-East, John Haswell House, 8–9 Gladstone Terrace, Gateshead NE8 4DY. £9.

WIN Directory Wales Council for Voluntary Action, Crescent Road, Caerphilly, Mid-Glamorgan CF8 1XL. £10.

About CAF

CAF, Charities Aid Foundation, is a registered charity with a unique mission – to increase the substance of charity in the UK and overseas. It provides services that are both charitable and financial which help donors make the most of their giving and charities make the most of their resources.

Many of CAF's publications reflect the organisation's purpose: *Dimensions of the Voluntary Sector* offers the definitive financial overview of the sector, while the *Directory of Grant Making Trusts* provides the most comprehensive source of funding information available.

As an integral part of its activities, CAF works to raise standards of management in voluntary organisations. This includes grants made by its own Grants Council, sponsorship of the Charity Annual Report and Accounts Awards, seminars, training courses and the Charities' Annual Conference, the largest regular gathering of key people from within the voluntary sector. In addition, Charitynet is now established as the leading Internet site on voluntary action.

For decades, CAF has led the way in developing tax-effective services to donors and these are now used by more than 150,000 individuals and 2,000 of the UK's leading companies; many are also using CAF's CharityCard, the world's first debit card designed exclusively for charitable giving. For charities, CAF's unique range of investment and administration services includes the CafCash High Interest Cheque Account, two common investment funds for longer term investment and a full appeals and subscription management service.

However, CAF's activities are not limited to the UK and, increasingly, CAF is looking to apply the same principles and develop similar services internationally, in its drive to increase the substance of charity across the world.

Charities Aid Foundation
Kings Hill
West Malling
Kent ME19 4TA

Telephone +44 (0) 1732 520000
Fax +44 (0) 1732 520001
E-mail cafpubs@CAF.charitynet.org
Web page http://www.charitynet.org

CAF publications

The Directory of Grant Making Trusts 1997–98 15th edition
ISBN 1859340253 £69.95 (2 volumes)
Published February 1997

Acknowledged as the definitive guide to grant-making trusts in the UK, this directory enables fundraisers to pinpoint those trusts whose funding objectives match their own particular project or area of work.

Split into two volumes for the first time, and containing the details of over 500 additional trusts, the 1997–98 edition has undergone a complete design overhaul in order to make the information it contains even more straightforward and accessible.

The indices which 'drive' the trust data have also been radically improved and an entirely new classification of types of beneficiary has been adopted. Particularly significantly, the listing of trusts by beneficial area has been reorganised in order to highlight regional funding preferences more clearly.

These improvements will enable fundraisers to obtain an even more detailed understanding of the future funding policies of the trusts listed and thereby to tailor their requests for support more accurately – reducing the time and money wasted on inappropriate appeals.

Grant-making trusts made grants in excess of £700m in 1995. The *DGMT* is designed to act as the lifeline between good causes in desperate need of support and this rich vein of funding.

Grantseeker The interactive CD-ROM for fundraisers
ISBN 1859340326   £150.00 + £26.25 VAT
Published February 1997

Drawing on CAF's years of experience as publisher of *The Directory of Grant Making Trusts*, Grantseeker is the tailor-made solution to the information needs of trust fundraisers in the electronic age.

Fully interactive, the specially designed search engine will scan the entire *DGMT* database in a matter of seconds on the basis of a user's own selection criteria and generate a ranked 'hit list' of trusts whose funding preferences match their project or cause. Selection criteria particular to the CD include details of grant size and grant type.

Taking full advantage of the 'added value' available via an electronic search tool, *Grantseeker* offers a more sophisticated matching service than can be provided by traditional methods, enabling fundraisers to save weeks of effort and frustration. A simple hypertext link can provide them with the complete directory entry on a potential funder within moments of loading the CD. The days of ultimate dependence on a paper-based directory are over.

The sample grants data from selected trusts, published separately in the *Grants Index*, appears in the full trust entries featured in *Grantseeker*.

Designed for use by fundraisers with little or no experience of electronic directories, as well as the more technically minded, *Grantseeker* provides step-by-step instructions on every stage of the search process backed by comprehensive help files. Even the most confirmed Luddite should not be intimidated!

Grantseeker runs under Windows 3.1 or Windows 95.

The Directory of Grant Making Trusts
Focus Series: Trustees Index

ISBN 1859340393 £14.95
Published January 1997

The importance of establishing 'who knows who' at an early stage in a fundraising campaign is widely recognised. In certain circumstances, a quiet word in an appropriate ear can be worth dozens of well-researched applications for support. And privately most grant-seekers acknowledge that some of their biggest donations are received from trusts where a trustee is personally known to a member of their appeal committee.

The Trustees Index provides an alphabetical listing of all the trustees whose names are held on the main database along with details of the trusts with which they are associated. Designed to be highly accessible, fundraisers will find it easy to use the directory to identify the details of particular individuals and use the data revealed to develop their own 'hit list' of trusts to be approached.

The Directory of Grant Making Trusts
Focus Series: Grants Index

ISBN 1859340261 £14.95
Published January 1997

Experienced grant-seekers know that whilst a large number of trusts may state that they are open to applications for support from organisations working in many different fields, there are many which, in reality, make donations only to particular causes.

Published as a companion volume to *The Directory of Grant Making Trusts*, the *Grants Index* provides comprehensive information on actual grants leading trusts have made in the recent past. Based on information received from the trusts themselves, the sample data provided is intended to be representative of the range of all the donations made.

Used in alliance with the relevant entry in the main directory, the *Grants Index* will enable fundraisers to build a more detailed profile of individual trusts and consequently target their applications more accurately.

The Directory of Grant Making Trusts
FOCUS SERIES: **Children and Youth**
ISBN 1859340172 £19.95
Published July 1996

The Directory of Grant Making Trusts
FOCUS SERIES: **Environment, Animal Welfare and Heritage**
ISBN 1859340164 £19.95
Published July 1996

Designed to make the search for funds easier still, many directories from the *Focus Series* will collect together, in individual volumes, details of trusts which have expressed an intention to support charitable activity in particular fields.

These directories, the first to appear, focus on trusts supporting causes associated with **Children and Youth** and **Environment, Animal Welfare and Heritage** projects. In addition to comprehensive details of the future funding priorities of the trusts listed, information is also provided on recent grants they have made.

Following the design established for the new-look *Directory of Grant Making Trusts*, these two directories will give grant-seekers working in the relevant fields a head-start in identifying sympathetic trusts and presenting well-tailored funding applications.

The Directory of International Funding Organisations
A guide for the non-profit sector
ISBN 1859340318 £19.95
Published December 1996

Fundraising outside our national borders is still an unknown quantity for many charities. This directory lists over 200 international funding organisations open to applications from voluntary organisations in the UK.

Each entry provides full details on:
- the scope of the funding programme
- the areas of activity for which funding is available

- restrictions and special requirements
- the principal beneficial areas within the UK
- application procedures and contact details

A series of tailor-made indices, based on those developed for the 1997–98 edition of *The Directory of Grant Making Trusts*, signposts users around the data to the funding source which most closely matches their needs.

CAF 'How to' Guides

A series of one-stop guides on a variety of core activities, the titles appearing in the CAF 'How To' series are designed to provide both volunteers supporting smaller charities – in either an official or an unofficial capacity – and inexperienced salaried staff with practical information and guidance on good practice.

> **Running a Local Fundraising Campaign** A guide for small voluntary organisations *Janet Hilderley*
> ISBN 1859340407 £9.95
> *Published April 1997*

For many small charities or regional branches a successful local fundraising campaign can generate lasting results not only in terms of the money raised but also in terms of enhanced public awareness of an organisation's existence and core activities. However, the work involved in planning and running a campaign can be considerable and there are undoubted risks if anything goes wrong.

It was once believed that it was possible to apply the same basic strategy developed for a national campaign to a local situation. Experience has proved that this approach seldom works and that greater account needs to be taken of local circumstances.

This guide provides practical information and advice on the enormous range of activities which can make up a local fundraising campaign and helps readers to assess which options would be most appropriate for their charity.

The Treasurer's Handbook A guide for small voluntary organisations *Ian Caulfeild Grant*

ISBN 1859340180 £7.95
Published August 1996

Recent legislation has reinforced the crucial role of the treasurer in voluntary organisations of all sizes, whilst the introduction of the SORP is intended to lead to a greater uniformity of practice throughout the sector.

As a treasurer's duties become more onerous, their personal, legal liability for the 'prudent management' of their organisation is thrown sharply into relief. Yet many volunteer treasurers do not have even a basic understanding of book-keeping activities.

In straightforward language, avoiding financial jargon, *The Treasurer's Handbook* outlines a treasurer's key tasks, proposes appropriate procedures and explains the basics of financial management.

Index

ACF *see* Association of Charitable Foundations

acknowledging cheques and letters 52

ACRE *see* Action with Communities in Rural England

ACTAF *see* Association of Community Trusts and Foundations

Action with Communities in Rural England (ACRE) 24, 58

aims and objectives (of projects):
    affinity with trusts' policies 28, 29, 40, 46–47, 51
    defining 28–29, 35–37, 40–41

annual reports 41, 53
    sponsorship of 41–42
    of trusts, as sources of information 16–17

appeals from abroad 20

applications, grant:
    and affinity with trusts' policies 28, 29, 40, 46–47, 51
    and defining projects 28–29, 35–37, 40–41
    deciding how much to ask for 34–35
    following trusts' guidelines 43, 44–45, 55
    and locally based trusts 13, 29, 30–31
    and targeting of trusts 29, 30, 32, *see* research
    see also letters, application

Association of Charitable Foundations (ACF) 56, 58

Association of Community Trusts and Foundations (ACTAF) 31, 58

CAF *see* Charities Aid Foundation

Carnegie United Kingdom Trust 11–12

'charitable purposes' 6–7

Charitable Trusts Administration Group 56

Charities Aid Foundation (CAF) 27, 44, 62–63
    see also Directory of Grant Making Trusts

Charities Digest 24

Charities Information Bureaux 27

Charity Commission Register 6, 7, 15, 22, 25, 26–27, 58

cheques, acknowledgement of 52

Children and Youth 24, 67

churches, role of 17

Citizens Advice Bureaux 17, 27

community-based projects 13, 29, 34

community trusts and foundations 30–31

companies, funding from 8, 9, 12, 30

'competition', assessing 15, 16–18, 41

computers, using 39–40, 45

'contributions', applying for 31, 33, 34

cooperation:
    with 'the competition' 18
    between trusts 35, 55–57

core funding, obtaining 34

corporate funding *see* companies, funding from

Councils for Voluntary Service (CVS) 17, 24, 27, 59

crises, grants in 37, 45

CVS *see* Councils for Voluntary Service

Directory of Grant Making Trusts (DGMT) 5, 11, 22–24, 28, 29, 30, 31, 42, 43, 49, 50, 60, 64
    Focus Series 24–25, 60, 66, 67
    Grantseeker 25, 60, 65

Directory of International Funding Organisations 67

Directory of Social Change (DSC) 25, 26, 27, 59

educational grants 20

emergencies, grants for 37, 45

emotive language 47

Environment, Animal Welfare and Heritage 24, 67

evaluation *see* monitoring and evaluation

extravagant claims 47–48

Fairness in Funding 56, 61

Family Welfare Association 24

Foundation Forum 55–56

FunderFinder 27, 28, 59
    FunderFinder for Individuals 27

funding of trusts:
    by central government 8, 9, 12
    by companies 8, 9, 12, 30
    by the general public 7–8, 9, 12, 13
    by local authorities 8, 9, 12

fundraisers, professional 33

geographical aspects 8, 13, 16, 30–31, 37

Gift Aid 8

gifts in kind 8, 29

GMT *see Guide to the Major Trusts*

grants:
    acknowledging 52
    as 'contributions' 31, 33, 34
    for core funding 34
    in emergencies 37, 45
    for innovative projects 12–13, 34
    size of 14, 31, 37
    monitoring and evaluation of 53–54
    'whole-project' and 'shopping list' approaches to 35
    see applications, grant

Grantseeker 25, 60, 65

Grants Index 24, 66

Guide to the Major Trusts (GMT) 25–26, 28, 31, 42, 61

'How to' Guides
    Running a Local Fundraising Campaign 68
    The Treasurer's Handbook 69

individual giving 7, 8, 9

individuals, grants to 20, 27

information, obtaining *see* research

innovative projects 12–13, 29, 34, 40

jargon, use of 46

letters, application:
    attracting attention with 19, 20
    bad English in 36, 43, 45–46
    duplicating 48
    emotive language in 47
    ending 47
    essential details in 36, 37, 40–41, 42
    essential enclosures for 41–42
    extravagant claims in 47–48
    following up 49–50
    headings of 38–39
    jargon in 46
    length of 40
    mentioning other trusts in 43
    over- and under-confident approaches in 46
    signatories to 42
    telephoning before sending 43
    and use of word processors 39–40, 45

letters, 'mailshot' 8, 19, 39, 45

local authorities 8, 17

local projects 13, 16, 29
local trusts, guides to 26, 30–31
location *see* geographical aspects
London Voluntary Services Council 27, 59
Lottery, the *see* National Lottery

'mailshot' letters 8, 19, 39, 45
meetings, trustees' 37, 45, 50
monitoring and evaluation 41, 52
   by trusts 53–54

National Association of Councils for Voluntary Service (NACVS) 24, 59
National Lottery 8
   Charities Board 13, 16
Northern Ireland trusts 6

objectives (of projects) *see* aims

patrons, co-opting 38–39
payroll giving scheme 8
'political correctness' 46
postage costs 19, 42
progress reports 53, *see also* monitoring and evaluation
'pump priming' 12

rejections 43, 50–51
research:
   importance of 17, 18, 21, 32
   into 'the competition' 15, 16–18, 41
   into trusts 13, 15, 16–17, 22–27
Running a Local Fundraising Campaign 68

Scottish Charities Office 6
seminars 22, 27, 44, 56
settlors 6
statutory funding 8, 9, 12
student applications 19, 20

targeting of trusts 28–31, 32, *see* research
tax 11
telephoning trusts 43, 50
Telethon 13
Treasurer's Handbook, The 69
Trustees Index 24, 66
trusts 6–7
   annual reports of 16–17
   community 30–31
   cooperation between 35, 55–57
   funding of *see* funding
   and innovative projects 12–13, 29, 34
   monitoring and evaluation by 53–54
   older 11–12
   proactive and reactive 14
   researching 13, 15, 16–17, 22–27
   and size of grants 14, 31
   small 13, 30, 31, 34
   targeting 28–31, 32
   and 'unpopular' causes 12, 13
   visits from officers of 43, 52, 53

videos, use of 42
visits, trustees' 43, 52, 53
Voluntary Organisation Liaison Officers 17
voluntary sector:
   getting information on 17
   sources of income 9

West Yorkshire Charities Information Bureau 27
word processors, using 39–40, 45
workshops 22, 27, 44